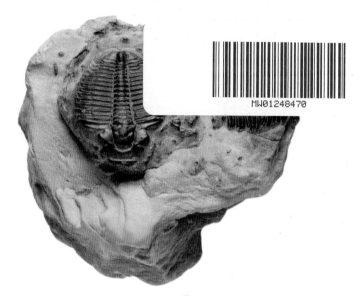

Fossils

by June Edelstein

Table of Contents

What Are Fossils?

Fossils are what is left of animals or plants that lived long ago. Here are **dinosaur** bone fossils. These bones were left behind when a dinosaur died. Over time, they turned into rock.

There are many different kinds of fossils.
There are fossils of teeth and bones.

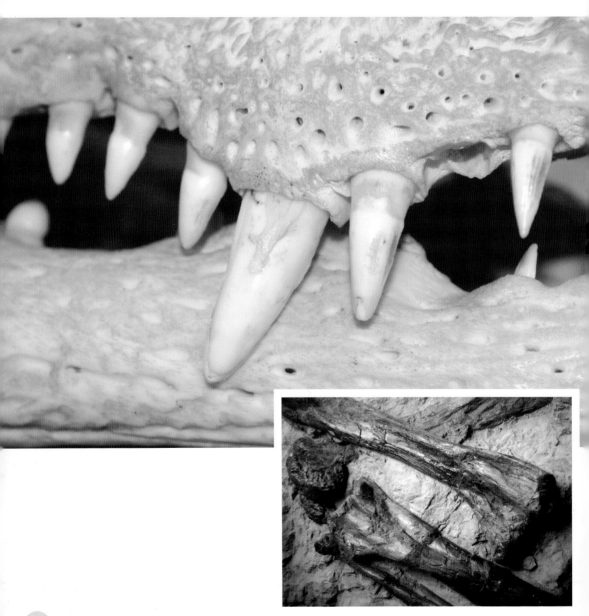

There are fossils
of footprints.

There are fossils
of shells and plants.

5

How Are Fossils Made?

Sometimes an animal dies in the water.

water

sand and clay

Soon, only the bones and teeth of the animal are left. Over time, sand and clay cover the bones and teeth.

water

sand and clay

After a long time, the water dries up. The bones turn into rock. This is how some fossils are made.

sand and clay

Often fossils are not the exact **remains** of plants and animals. Instead, they are marks left behind by plants and animals. These marks are usually made in mud. The mud hardens into rock.

A leaf left its outline on this rock.

What Things Can Fossils Tell Us?

Fossils tell us things about the past.
Fossils tell us how animals looked
long ago. This is a fossil of a bird.
How is it like the birds we see today?

This is the fossil of a bird
from **prehistoric** times.
It is called **archaeopteryx**.

The fossils we find help us make **models** of how animals used to look. This dinosaur was much bigger than a child. This dinosaur was much bigger than a car. It was even bigger than an elephant!

14

Fossils tell us how animals lived long ago. Fossils of footprints tell us if an animal walked on two or four legs. They can tell us if the animals moved around together or moved alone.

These are fossils of footprints. Animals made these footprints when they walked in the mud. What do these fossils tell us about the animal that made them?

Over the years, the mud hardened into rock to make these fossils of animal footprints.

Fossils tell us how the earth
has changed over the years.
Sometimes you can find fossils
of seashells on the top of a mountain.

These fossils tell us that the mountain
used to be under the ocean!

What might have happened to make the ocean
so far from the mountains?

How Do We Find Fossils?

People find fossils in many different ways. Sometimes people look for fossils in the sand or mud. Sometimes rocks must be opened to find fossils.

These scientists are on a **dig**. They are opening rocks to look for dinosaur fossils.

Sometimes people find fossils by chance.
They may find fossils
when they are digging in the earth
to build a road or a house.

Anyone can find a fossil.
Just keep your eyes open.

Glossary

archaeopteryx (ar-kee-AHP-tuh-riks): a prehistoric bird that looked like a reptile

dig (DIG): a search for fossils

dinosaur (DY-nuh-sor): a reptile that lived millions of years ago

fossils (FAH-sulz): what is left of animals or plants that lived long ago

models (MAH-dulz): things built to show what the real objects might look like

prehistoric (pree-is-TOR-ik): from a time before history was written down

remains (rih-MANEZ): parts left behind by plants or animals

Index

20